TIME'S BODY

ALSO BY DABNEY STUART

Poetry

The Diving Bell
A Particular Place
The Other Hand
Round and Round: A Triptych
Rockbridge Poems
Common Ground
Don't Look Back
Narcissus Dreaming
Light Years: New and Selected Poems
Second Sight: Poems for Paintings by Carroll Cloar
Long Gone
Settlers
The Man Who Loves Cézanne
Family Preserve
Tables
Greenbrier Forest

Fiction

Sweet Lucy Wine
The Way to Cobbs Creek
No Visible Means of Support

For Children

Friends of Yours, Friends of Mine
Open the Gates

Criticism

Nabokov: The Dimensions of Parody

TIME'S BODY

New and Selected Poems
1994–2014

BY

DABNEY STUART

PINYON PUBLISHING
Montrose, Colorado

Cover Photograph: Annular solar eclipse, Chaco Canyon, New Mexico,
May 20, 2012, by Stan Honda

Photograph of Dabney Stuart by Emily Smith

Book and Cover Design by Susan E. Elliott

First Edition: March 2014

Pinyon Publishing
23847 V66 Trail, Montrose, CO 81403
www.pinyon-publishing.com

Library of Congress Control Number: 2014903289
Stuart, Dabney 1937 –
ISBN: 978-1-936671-22-9

Acknowledgments

Some of the new poems here previously appeared in:

The Georgia Review ("The Judge at Work"); *The Hampden-Sydney Poetry Review* ("The Elephant"); *Pinyon Review* ("Bird," "Revisiting *Partial Accounts* in Italy," "Time's Body," "Office"); *Alhambra Poetry Calendar, 2010* ("Bric-a-Brac"); *Alhambra Poetry Calendar, 2011* ("Drought: October"); *Alhambra Poetry Calendar, 2013* ("Greenbrier Forest").

The selected poems are from the following volumes, with the permission of the author:

Long Gone, (LSU Press, Baton Rouge, LA, 1996); *Settlers* (LSU Press, Baton Rouge, LA, 1999); *The Man Who Loves Cézanne* (LSU Press, Baton Rouge, LA, 2003); *Tables* (Pinyon Publishing, Montrose, CO, 2009).

For Sandra

and for my children:

Nathan, Darren, and Martha (1961-2000)

Nothing's going to grow if it's not there.

—André Viette

Consciousness caps her life
by considering it, and talking to
itself about absent parts of it.

—George Santayana

CONTENTS

TIME'S BODY

ONE

TWO

THREE

FOUR

TIME'S BODY

ONE

TO BODY GONE

The whole of things: the settling mind
filters to the chest and loins,
as from one place the heart can send
its fretting to the farthest veins.

My mind sings in my foot, my hip,
my knuckle's bulb, my popliteal.
It is my body's netted sap,
a keeping and a carousel.

Its famous rising to abstruse,
regardless smoke and show
turns downward to the place it grows,
contents itself with wrist and toe,

articulates a fuller art
than brain alone can perpetrate—
towered, capped in its bone, apart.
Descent is more commensurate.

I tell you this in confidence
since more than a skip of fear attends.
I take it slow. I do this dance
in the marrow and the little bones.

A TRUE STORY

Time, my miniature stone
gargoyle, sits on the table
beside me, keeps his secret.
I don't ask him for anything
beyond his presence, touch
his head, trace my fingertip
lightly down his nose,
a panther's nose.
I have felt an essence, a still
thrive, pass through the forehead
of a Great Dane—regal, high-strung—
into mine; kneeling, I held
her bowed head between my hands,
fingers along her jaws, her face
too close to see clearly,
our foreheads all
but melded. My forefinger
touches Time's head like that,
draws away slowly
and is still attached to my hand.

WOODS CREEK TRAIL

1

At the second bridge over the trail
the many-layered shadows recede;
an illusion of openness opens.

Near it, the bankside jewelweed's tiny
leopards breathe fire until I glance back
and the dew glints its thousand-eyed trick.

On a pine branch, within reach, a catbird shrugs.

The fear adrift always in my breathing wanes;
my foot's hushed chuff on the packed dirt blends
with crow music and a sparrow's trim flight.

2

In the short stone tunnel under the footbridge
the creek takes on a stillness, gives no sign
it will spill into white riffles leaving,
curving toward the last ford in the stretch
before the trail bends toward the cliffs.

From up there it's impossible to see
the thistledown catch on the air, and fall.

3

Water throughover the long ledges,
wood chips darkened in low mist,
time thinning;
                along the aisle of pines
silverlight shimmers in the high needles,
flying in place.

I imagine an air I can breathe through my pores,
imagine a breathing altogether.

The pattern of rising and falling
I see the world in fades, replaced
by a radiance, a windblown lightness
in the place, in me, absorbing.

SOLO

When the oboist turned the page
of her music, the quick shadow
of her hand touched the tip

of the oboe's shadow on her dress,
about knee-high on the silk folds.

Those shadows played with her,
their motions oddly syncopated
with the sway of her body

as she drew breath and gave it
to the light-stunned tube she fingered,
otherwise empty. Her music,

sinuous as swallow flight,
emptied the mind, too.
Nothing became

the way it floated, its local air,
swallowed by nothing.
She followed a trail of notes,

but her listeners
went off into myriad lost
meanders, keeping

almost no time. They knew
nothing, did not think
about form and void, or anything

on the face of the earth
or moving upon its waters.
Instead, they took heart

from this wind blowing them away.

A LITTLE GIRL TOUCHES MY SLEEVE

Heavy men in plaid shirts
are punching out the riverfront
cop behind the warehouses.
The smell of curing tobacco
and piss permeates the mist.
I want to help him, to drag
the meaty thugs off him
and throw them into the river,
but I am only the dreamer.
The echo of his body absorbing
the dull blows thickens the air;
to this beat I wave the townspeople
off the dirt street, into their homes.
A slow shift, a tide, draws them back
to the storefronts, and then pulls
them down the board steps
into the street. I feel
their mounting cheer, their eagerness,
their taking into themselves
the dark bodies of violence
at the edge of their knowing.
They gaze as one body themselves
downhill toward the quay, watching
the line of white limousines rise
slowly toward us: streamers,
tossed flowers, a shimmering
of air and voices in the tableau.
A round-faced, glittering little girl
touches my sleeve. Without speaking,
she whispers in the silence
of the packed street, the suspended cortege,

Perhaps it will be a cleansing of the family.
I want to ask her what family,
what gathering of people may lead me
to the body of my letting go.
But she's not there. Nothing is there.

LUIS APARICIO

In my head he still lifts without effort
off the skinned dirt at deep short,
sails gracefully, his legs tucked up,
a bird ascending, toward the soft liner
also sailing in the softly misted air
over the clipped green infield toward center.
Two drifting outfielders compose a backdrop,
spectators, too, of this impeccable tableau.
We become, all of us, suspended in our rows
of concentric awe, dispossessed by time,
watching Luis's ineffable pantomime
gather its ghosts—Concepción, Rizzuto,
Carrasquel, and, for its faintest aura,
Russ Kern, shimmering in contours around him.
The ball hovers; all the Luises hover,
absorbed, none of them as intimate
with each other as with the immanent dot
of perspective where they will never meet.

THE JUDGE AT WORK

The ash on her cigar
hasn't fallen, though she still
smokes after all these years.
It extends over a mile now—
from her high, austere
bench down the courtroom aisle,
out the double walnut doors
kept open in all weather
for the sake of this sheer
incomparable stupor,
past the squat statue
of the oblivious hero's smile
by the water fountain,
across Main Street whose traffic
has long been mazily diverted
elsewhere, through the abandoned
Woolworth's (its letters golden
still above the blank plate glass),
and so on to the mythic
edge of town, suspended
there like a ramrod
waiting for its barrel,
or, if you come toward it head-
on, a burnt-out eye deeper
than lineage or culture.
Not even the winos marvel
anymore at what's come to pass
through their dilapidated
park—they manage to duck
under it blotto, are
unfazed by its non-bibulous

14

spirit level, neither bar
nor horizon, but in their
skewed view appropriate
somehow. Less addlepated,
joggers simply re-route.
No one seems to remark
the small cries, vaguely angelic,
that also hover sometimes
around the whim of the law,
little choruses of mercy once called for
under its wide panoply.
Whatever hypnotic effect
this slow growth had on the jury
became long ago moot;
we have come to accept,
just so, the judge at work—
salutary, incorrupt—
keeping the thin band of flame
glowing, her verdict enacting itself
in the fine stretch of waste
shaping the way we are.

REPLACING THE SURFACE

How heavily he lies on the couch,
or seems to, seems to sink into it,
become the element that supports him,
a giving like a swimmer's to water.
It's not easy to say how long he's been here,
or how long it takes for the body
to discover the eye of the storm,
the primary junction of rest and motion.
If he died here and lay unattended
the blood would pool in his down side,
postmortem lividity showing something
of his true longing, his body's inner dream.
T'ai chi stresses a lowering
of the center of gravity—chest to abdomen—
for balance, a truer center, a tug
against the pride of the cerebrum.

So we imagine his heart stops.
He sleeps an old sleep, untroubled, his peace
purely physical, an end to tending:
frequently stitched up, his scars little medals
of time stood off; wearing next to his rings
three small doilies of polyethylene mesh,
demure barriers against the spilling
of his guts; carrying along his spine—
that high-rise condo timeshare for posh
viruses—the ripe old chicken pox,
its cousin Zoster with the Nietzschean name,
and who knows what other indestructible
rentiers with their feet up on the table
until their next foray into the neighborhood;

typhus' long-drawn issue whispering
in his blood, memory and cellular
recurrence muddled like the weather report
and actual rain in the next county;
scopes in at both ends, like lovers seeking
against all obstacles to meet
in the darkened alley for that kiss
worth dying for; and, not last or least,
O neuritis rara, the viral expedition
that planted its beige flag in his left eye,
giving new meaning to the phrase
to look around. Here, in the intimate,
distressed body of it, his history
stops, too. Not even the most precisely skilled
forensic pathologist could see more deeply
into the finished man than we do,
watching him virgin dead on the flat couch.

Consider disease as a chameleonic ruse.
Time looks at the sick man, sees him begin
to blend into circumstance like ripe fruit
into puree, senses his will disperse
into the grand Lucretian welter, and turns
its immediate attention elsewhere,
letting the poor bugger be, alone
with his brief reprieve, flipping the old saying
on its head: *You can hide, but you can't run.*
Recovery, then, becomes a return
to the more normal scrutiny revolving us
minutely on its spit until we're done.

We don't see him move, but a figure rises
from his figure, sinuous as smoke
from a camp fire, oblivious to anything
but its own motion, the way it would contrive
to make shape of its waywardness, and settle—
so quickly transient it nudges
time's membrane. And yet each instant
elongates as if it were almost endless,
now and *forever* the impossible reflections
of each other, absolute compression
coterminous with the widest opening out.
Now its right arm stretches away, languidly
almost, to the side, easy in the elbow,
thumb and fingers touching at their tips,
the hand forming a kind of bird's head, its bill
dipping for water in the air; he turns
his body away from this, leaving it
to its unseen pitch, bringing his left hand
up before him, softly angled, palm out, a greeting
and a fending off. Such weightless faith
in the pending derivation of what comes next
becomes his temper, the way he lives now.

Two

WRITING A BOOK

—the longest
odds, a loss of life
in the twining. Who survives it,
leaves.

The words say *Here*,
but they dance *Goodbye*,
an enhancement, echoes
of no one.

There, the writer says,
nunc dimittis, going his way
out of them,
humming the void.

He waves at the sounds
which kept him
alive toward the nowhere
they disperse into,

his bearing.

THE ELEPHANT

The elephant whirls his rippling body
round and round my study, filling it
with his bloat, his drive. When he's like this
I wish he was in the zoo, or just being
his implausible self on an old plain
in the proud bulge of west Africa.
He fills the room in the same way
we say the heart fills the throat
in moments of grief, or elation.
There's still space for me at my desk
or in the rocker beside the small table,
but I feel altogether displaced.
There is hardly air in the air
around his sudden matter. He cavorts.
He enjambs. His incomprehensible trunk
rises and writhes, lies listless along his head,
explores his ridiculously pert lip
as if he were puzzled to find himself
in a place never divulged to him
in the embedded codes of his past.
Dumbo he could have been, a kite flying,
its colorful leash stretched between him
and the fickle tyke who in a moment
of inattention would let him go.
But this summoning, this conscription?
After he had settled into a tidy rumination,
done with embodiments thrust on him
by these creatures who sit half the time
because they have only two legs? Who are they
with their isolate musters, their dry blames,
those absurd bulbs at the top of their bones?

I could empathize even further—
that's what a study's for, to enter
the other presences who haven't succumbed
to your version of them—but he nuzzles
me, mashes me against the book shelves
so the titles of two or three volumes
imprint my neck, turns his haunch into me
as if this whole enterprise were a dance.
I've lost track of how often he appears
on my desk from nowhere, a statuette
for the vacant hours, bad penny.
I reach out to touch him with my finger,
feather along the spine—never mind
I know what comes next, how he bursts
into full-blown performance.
He presses me into the farthest corners
until my skin seems laminate with his;
I am spread so thin he could read the spines
of my books through me, if he could read.
But he's content to strut and arabesque,
elaborate his mischief until, at the instant
of my dispersal, he vanishes,
leaving me where I've been all our lives.
He's here, of course, even when he's not
his two extremes, the walls and ceiling
his shape my study, our little everywhere.

AN OLD STONE SAVAGE, ARMED

He walks Main Street, a book in each hand,
arms swinging gently, a modest stride.
The titles change week by week,
but his purpose is constant—*Read*—
no tv, or palm-sized distractions
held to the ear. He follows where the brute
need of another life leads him, letter by letter.

After he leaves the library, elbow to the glass door,
and takes on the fraught shade of the Main St. trees,
he probably doesn't remark the Sushi bar,
or the barber shop with its antiquated pole—
the chirurgeon's bloody clouts—still spiraling,
or the cemetery where famous people are buried.

He turns onto a rick of side streets,
balanced against odds, his fingertips
already intimate with the dust jackets:
that the halves of the brain could be so balanced,
words and numbers weighing each other
in the same scale, a synaptic dance
as cogent as he is. His way home

into pages he may well have lived through before
takes him finally into a smaller maze
of alleys, graveled, weedy, until he finds
a door that seems familiar. Shifting
the weight he has borne at arms' length
to the grip of elbow against side,
he opens it. He sets the books down
on the table beside the chair he reads in.

He closes the door. He sits himself down.

The book he opens nestles into the hand,
open also, that seems designed to hold it—
spine across the palm, in the thumb crease,
fingers hefting the weight of the future.
There's nothing for him to know, only a voice
making its way through an untold jungle of letters,
arranging, patterning, letting it happen.
He closes his eyes. He listens.
When he's ready, he turns the page.

PSALM

Tenses are a loss,
the lungs' ash,
their lament.

The winged euonymus, on fire,
does not sum up,
or the hemlock, deepening.

Dust is a paradise,
air's shuttlecock,
its scatter and nest.

It's the diamond's joy
to have faults, the earth's,
along which to shatter,
open.

Light is a match for this,
breaking, threading
its needle.

MATTER

When I wrote those lines
about double exposures, and wept to read them,
I was looking over a port on Akaroa
toward Rangitoto, one street down
from the rose gardens where a pohutukawa
cast its red blossoms against the season,
hearing the multisyllabic patter
of Pacific tongues confound wind and weather.
From there to McMurdo is a short declension—

the deeper south, the ambience of space
at its outer reaches set on my own planet
spinning in its unpredictable orbit.
I like to sing off key about space,
my inner harbor no longer set apart
from Alpha Centauri or more distant
configurations, no longer a retreat.
Words become, besides coagulates of space,
signals I pick up, sheer impulses

I listen for, choose, tune—the finest matter
making air of itself, itself of air.
They become as they drift beyond echo
what I understand *nothing* might refer to,
a new version of the music of the spheres,
set in a visual sea like stars burning
their stunned transformations, their undertow
sometimes so fierce they consume themselves, careers
spun to a vacuum blackbright in its turning.

So, reading, I wept. An old sorrow rose
with the words, an intimate sounding shaped
and turned to air no longer secret from me.
For years I had breathed this without release;
now *that* mystery inhered in this one
and I in both of them, and the wider dream
of language, its boisterous sprawl, overlapped
and shattered, a starry void, almost a clone
of the mist filling the harbor, or my voice.

BIRD

Another poet had a tall tree
in his ear. I have a crow.
We are similarly imbalanced
but my figure sings.

It can't carry a tune,
disdains harmony,
keeps words at bay.

In its own way, sings.

REVISITING *PARTIAL ACCOUNTS* IN ITALY

for William Meredith (1919-2007)

There's a lot of inventive praise for you
and your art on the jacket of your book:
"If poetry were landscape," one writer says,
"this work would be a national park."

Well, that trope makes you vast and wildly diverse,
which you weren't, but the trek
so many take, say, to Yellowstone
they would make as rewardingly to your book.

I have made such a trip—two trips in one,
in the manner of *my* trope here, in fact—
to Bellagio, where I've found your book,
and your poem about this equivocal place.

The shade of your self you watched wander the park
below you has long since merged with your verse.
Those fishermen whose bells beguiled your dark
have been replaced by pleasure boats, but the stars

continue to work their netting, magical
above the cypresses. One could still get caught,
willy-nilly, in the cold but lyrical
clues they may, or may not, offer for our art.

They hang in deep blue space, indifferent,
finally, to the odd coracle
in which we drift, local and intent,
figuring what we love, discovering how

a book may be a place where we can at least
settle something of what the world disposes
us to shy away from, the scattered pieces
we gather into the haven of a voice.

BRIC-A-BRAC

Another bloody Suffering Irish Author,
saying nothing and everything,
her story going round and round itself,
a carousel, cotton candy making,
a black hole sucking the world in.
We ought to take up a collection.
It's the music, surely, that seduces us,
helps us through the plethora of details
which would otherwise bore us silly
or suffocate us like a thousand pillows
held to our faces. The music is
the only perspective, the way to endure
the overstuffed parlor that is the book,
and the island; it's what makes bearable
how small it all is, and getting smaller,
closing in on its own repetition.
And above it all perches the myopic,
smug little icon, wizened, as in life,
his eyes a rumor behind the bottle-
thick lenses of his granny specs.
It's fitting that his name rhymes with *voice*,
though the ones who've come after him, buried
in his routine of small bits, have a better
ear than he did, for all his penny poems.
Regardless of their disparate efforts
to shake loose, to exorcise their *Da*,
they carry him along, willy nilly,
extending his colossal joke—almost,
now, a hundred years of lilting failure,
an homage shooting itself in the foot.

This is how the populace—the part that reads—
talks to itself, manages the humdrum,
arranges the scraps of household nostalgia
on the rickety table, the top of the spinet.
There's a knitted, skirtlike thingie hanging
from the ceiling fixture, the fringe of which
brushes your forehead when you walk through.

DRAWING

*Is the existence of spirit evident
to spirit, and involved in the presence
of anything?*
　　　　　　　—George Santayana

Neither the grain in the stone
nor the pigment in the columbine
cares if the chisel or brush
works its long-range intimation.
My heart aches or doesn't ache
depending on what language one prefers,
but when the afternoon light hits river stone
in a wall and draws out its peach undertone,
its violet rhythm, something in my chest
empties itself into my fingers.
How this is inevitably lost
composes one history of art, an out take
skittering in the wind, nostalgia's rush.

Wordsworth said despondency and madness
are what we poets come to, and floated off
into vacancy. Words failed him, too,
or left him to himself, as paint does,
absorbing what passes through the painter:
art not as detritus, or a record of failure,
but as a new body for the spirit's life,
though it's as empty hanging before you
as any artist contorted by the throes
of passage, or as you are, looking. Distress
and disconnection spread their random dust
into our breathing, a more likely wake
of the body's long draw into the future.

A child's hand hovering at my shoulder
once created in the space between us
a place full of itself, ghosting, an air.
We didn't touch, but touch happened there,
our emptiness and no one's, suspending art
in the stroke of its beginning. Color,
contour, texture, composition blended
into nothing, or became its semaphore.
Her hand seemed to levitate apart
from breath or body, anything intended.
Nearness and distance were coterminous,
names for the draft between, the passing space
not even imperious thought can enter.

The poem opens only when consciousness
relents, disperses into the true mist
of mind delighting in itself, in nothing
rising. In the rare instants of arrest—
rifts in our knowing—when art meets time,
binding their traces into a tandem stress
of light and echo, all striving releases,
becomes an entrance to its giving ground.
Settling, we could call it, or water bathing
motionless in a depth we cannot sound
otherwise: a receding shadow, a name
feathering. Gravity and air may kiss
here, too, sketching their implicit dream.

Cézanne said everything we look at vanishes.
His pigments bound hard light into the canvas,
bore plane after plane into each other,
a tectonic shifting that still touches
the deep plates, moves mountains to regather,
makes the heart ache and the fingers tremble,
never at peace in their constricted reaches.
An embodiment troubled in its body
mocks the eye, makes the painting seem to crumble,
iotas of inkling scattered in the iris:
the act of sight itself becomes unsteady.
And yet it doesn't move. Nothing moves. A trace
of something softening the air diminishes.

In the midst of art time keeps, its moment
opened to nothing, a likely space—
spidery facades, faces, a tilted balance
of apple and cloth, of arches, a slight mirage,
a feint of offings, their shadowy cadence—
in every instance blending, inherent.
A life which passes into its own midst
kin to that opening does not release
anything from the painting's immanence,
but may stand before it like the child's hand
ghosting my shoulder, enabling presence.
Pigment and stone and word absorb a passage
rising through surfaces, spindrift in the mind

dispersing, a vacancy of limitless
incomprehension. This is different
from ecstasy, or a scoured vision where otherness
clarifies, or even long familiar
habits dwindling into their semblances.
Letting go, we could call this phase, the shapes
of water and shadow opening to thin air,
spaceless, unmediating. Nothing is born
here. Disconnection and despondency,
near and far, fade into the diaphane.
Empty and empty merge, voiding synapse,
a last resort: and spirit no longer gropes,
verging, into the next brush stroke, the next line.

THREE

VIGIL

I kneel beside her,
touching my fingertips to a vein:
her heartbeat, and the wane of life.
The little pool at the back
of my mind, our past,
ripples with my breathing,
the edge of everything.

The air thins;
around my brittle tinder,
the surface of heat my body is,
it is full of unlikeness.

Through the pool's surface
 a bird rises, the eye of time, fledged,
dripping with aspiration.
It spins slowly, suspends itself.

I turn into its flying.

LOVE TRIANGLE

The woman shading her eyes
looks across the grass
at the child smiling at the photographer
focusing his lens on the woman's bare legs.
They are fine legs, one extended
toward the photographer, helping
to balance her, the other crossed over it
just above the knee. One doesn't know
how she moved following this snapshot,
or how many more frames he exposed.
Patience may have been rewarded.
The child is full of elation, bursting,
an extension of the raft of yellow flowers
surrounding her and the woman
intent upon her. As if to intensify
the sunlight around them, muting the flowers,
they sit in a peninsula of shadow.
The woman marks an edge of this, her arm up,
her hand—a dancer's hand—casting
a lighter shadow over her eyes.
Of the photographer we know nothing
except the quality of his attention,
tied into this group as surely as the red swing
hanging from a cropped-out tree in the far
background is, stilled, an inclination.

THRESHOLD

A figure rises from its body's stillness—
a haze at first, tentative, appearing
as if by accident, a random drift
of air making air visible, a shape.

A haze at first, tentative, appearing
as if by magic, the figure waves
at air, making air visible, a shape
evolving toward itself. Amorphous, forming

as if by magic, the figure waves
a farewell or a greeting to the world
evolving toward itself. Amorphous, forming,
it gives no clue to what its gesture means:

a farewell or a greeting to the world
it leaves or enters. As it develops
it gives no clues to what its gestures mean
outside the world it shapes in its vague shifting.

It leaves or enters as it develops
space around it, certain of nothing
outside the world it shapes. In its vague shifting
it may not leave *or* enter, but abide.

Space around it, certain of nothing else,
becomes a giving way, becomes the life
it may not leave or enter, but abide
as a figure rising in its spirit's stillness

AN OLD MAN AND A SMALL CHILD

One of them looks into the camera,
not posing exactly, but loving
its impersonal caress. He's done this
before, already developing his face.
The other, holding the child, looks off
at an angle 90 degrees from the line
of the shot. It's likely he was
unaware of the little tick of light
signalling this instant. His skin is worn,
a leathery texture, sundown, contrasting
sharply with the child's pale, interior smoothness.
With his wide eyes he could be a putto
let loose from the cathedral ceiling
to spread his impish delight and mischief
among the supplicants. The old man seems
to be listening to something, lest it escape
his innate skepticism, his fond hope.
His gray chin whiskers barely graze the almost
golden hair of the little boy nestled
against his chest. Their visible hands—
the man's right spread on the boy's back, fingertips
toward the lens, the boy's curled into the man's
shirt—make a circle of the affection
inattentively running through them.
If their positions were reversed—the boy
in profile, the man face on—there'd be no hint
of where their mutual life comes from,
how it courses, how sufficient it is.
These two people, 70 years between them,
show no inclination to movement, no
interest in whatever happens next.

DROUGHT: OCTOBER

A dark tendency laces the cloud bank,
the hard stuff, water chaser to follow.
But these months the omens never open,
giving no more water than an oar drips,
feathering. Who imagines shades of brown
becomes a lord, his fiefdom gathering
in the gutters, layering on the crisp grass.
Children seem shadows of themselves,
playing at summer in this dreary wane.

One of them, a girl, broomstick skinny,
bobs on a trampoline, skewering air,
making a scattered skyline, random, gone
with every bounce gone. At the high instant
of each jump, as she starts down, her hair
flies up as if she is plummeting through water.
The sun streams in it.

Unseasonal the pundits call it,
but it's its own season, washing the borders
of hot and cold, lush and skeletal,
we measure the temperate years by.
Daily life becomes rote imitation,
a haunting yesterday that drifts from us
caught in our current vigil, hung in an air
between hoping and keeping time.

The leaves from a Japanese maple,
suddenly crimson, fall to a circle
of fire inside the drip line. They shrivel
into themselves, miniature fists curling.
I could place this small marvel, flamingly
modest, brief as rime, on the crest of a rise
in the western grasslands, back off from it
twenty miles or so, and watch the sun set

through it: fades of yellow and magenta
lined with navy and peach in its surrounding,
the trace of the rise sloping away
gently toward an abandoned pig farm.
This could be where we wait, on the prairie,
seared, stretching forever to its edges.
We could settle for nightfall. We could look up.
We could remember this is how it's been

always. Awakening to the burning bush
would become routine, one morning's answer
to another, a lively withering,
our neighborhood. Children scale ladders
of smoke, dive into pails of char, clamber
on jungle gyms so lithely they don't singe
their hands. We urge newcomers to be fruitful
and multiply under the festering sun.

The eventual locusts pass us by
as if *we* were a plague. Not even manna,
quick confetti, falls on our rubbled furrows.
But in this habit of mind, our Utopia,
clouds might flock drunkenly in the west,
pour toward us, unload rain on Wonderland.
Where would we be then?—trapped in a reverse
logic of our own making, longing for
our sere little acre under heaven.

The lean girl has gone in for supper.
A few last leaves float to the trampoline.
My neighbor's oak splits, carefully laid by,
have long since cured, their sap dissipated
to air. They will be little more than tinder
in the bleak months ahead. Nobody
sitting hearthside has heard quite so sharply
before, the crackling of the earth going dry.
To be warmed by it takes your breath away.

PLYING

Another thread blends into my mind,
my memory of it—if a memory—
like the spent dye water
drying in the sand where the woman
in the white apron and black shawl
poured it from her pot.
She hangs the indigo skeins
on porch pegs, and goes inside.
The flimsy screen door shuffles
against the threshold, nearly closed.
A rent in the lower right corner
curls inward. Following this thread
could be a way to recover
what her presence has become
part of, but I have only
a tenuous sense of how her dye
in the sand touches what I am
absorbing. Like the sand. The net
of the screen wire curling casts
shadows inward on the unswept floor.
By now the thread is fully meshed
in the words I speak, my being
able to speak, my being.
It's as if the woman never existed,
her dye in the windstilled sand
gone with the sand. I can't take
her roughened hand and stroke it,
can't thank her enough, can't unthread
her from the way I disappear into the weave.

THE SAME FINGER

In the kitchen, a year-old child
arcs her forefinger into the air,
the rise of spirit
a comma in the body's rush,
an attention.

So much awaits, so many ways
for her to mark the music
passing through her, so many
beckonings. For now, she continues
to forget her finger, looks
aside and down. The pattern
of the Belouch wavers
in the morning shadows, one of them
cast by the curve of her forehead.
She bows slightly to see it move.

She brings her hand
in to her chest, touching,
and then slowly lets it slip
to her side; her finger—
the same finger—straightens
toward her place in the shadow,
pointing.

BUSHEL

Matthew 5:15

Everything told him to keep his light to himself.

He thought at first his light might be a way
through this life, or out of it,
but that was before he understood
causality and friction; before the fear
of candor, the imbalance of precision
and language, were set before him
like a banquet he would best partake of
at an angle. *Veer* the manual said.
Shy. Distance became

his preferred place, his tending. A thin music
shredded over thorns, the reeds of fall whirred.
His voice played in his years like a humming
he tuned under his breath, the life of paintings
after the museum closes.
This was positive. This was *here*, his dance
of webs, his bravery in the foe's house,

his underhand. It wasn't ecstasy—
time's jig with light—but it was at least
a shadow of it, so he cavorted
until the latch clicked and the shiny toes
strode in. Lesson three: *keep moving*. The turns
and returns his voice wove were their own life now,
sounds he murmured like song titles,
twined along the radiant stretches

all of whose threads he could not follow at once.
Could he *be* the web and be on the web
in the same instant, the one life? If he could,
he couldn't know when he was; he had
only the echo of it to tell him so.
After a while, gone into the chases of air,
tempered by the rhythms of compression
and dispersal, measureless,

he understood it was the mesh that spoke,
the web its own music, which he no longer
sought to compose but to remain a part of,
to enter and re-enter, listening,
keeping time, or time's harmony with light
and the air in light, cantor and supplicant,
needing only to be in the whole range
of this transition he had begun
with the first threadnote of a word.

But he heard the world call, too,
scattering his attention, sprays of chance
and option asking for everything.
There was no pattern to it; the scree
of practicality spread where he walked.
He scuffed his shoes in it. He breathed *its* dust, too.
Its distraction frayed his mind, a tinnitus.
Could he wind *that* into his music?
Was this rattled, careless mime the counterpoint

of nothing, his neverlove, his shadowair?
His affection for it waxed and wavered,
a beat he would lean toward, hear his voice
toy with, feel edge into his light, the foe's house
opening its easy welcomes. His mistrust of it
sometimes seemed no more than a lapse
he could disappear into, another time.
The pressure was not to listen, but to keep
track, consider the beckonings, see who wanted
what by which importunate name.

And, as if that weren't enough,
his body spoke a language, too,
had its own way of rustling the network,
making its presence felt. It was the brother
of the world, but somehow also kin
to his light. Three riddles, nestling: his light
voice, the Siren world he had no call in,
his body which seemed its own vocation.

These riddles crossing were as inescapably *here*
as the distance he composed in his voice's weaves.
If his music were to sound its web truly
it would become the fire that consumes
everything, time's dance and speech igniting,
stars in their courses, books burning,
the flowers of Edo, isothermal,
a field of fireflies on a summer night.

52

Four

CHILDREN

A child appears in a room empty.
I turn away at the door,
thinking to let him be.
        Again.
Be with him, our voice says.
Sit with him in the years
our bewilderment begins
its long drift toward music,
our nets. Gather.

Otherwise you are a scatter of sounds,
no one.

No other.

NOT EVEN LIGHT

I make this moment
into you, have it speak.
God's absence fades briefly
behind our mist, words hung
over a black hole.
That other Incarnation
was no less miraculous.

So what the choir sings,
and *Hosanna* into the mist.
Sometimes morning is a chop
of bitterness into the neck,
more lessons in memory's dojo.

She who keeps me
in touch with my best self
is going on a long trip.
I'll wander around the house
listening to you for two weeks;
then she'll come back
with her welcoming voice,
and I'll be that much older.

Not even light fits.

MEAT MARKET

October 11. The doubling of a prime
into a prime. A leanness, mirrored.
Once, the number on my back.

Except for the calendar, you wouldn't know
such a day occurred in 1901.
No one could have foreseen it,
not even God, the mighty fraction.
I quail before his eye
in the peak of the pyramid,
shivering in my jungle of alphabets.

I saw myself in the cross hairs,
leveled, my heart a bilge pump.
Nobody dies all the time
said the Collector of Lint,
Get in line. I'd never known
what *age* meant, a hand
drilled into my sternum, hoisting me
onto the carcass rack, going round.

The calendar records it was a Thursday
—far enough back, near turning—
but not the stars in their courses
or space's unraveling, its binge.
Wherever fire beckons in a dark wood
time, too, disperses,
rapture in a circle of flies.

Meanwhile, scored by the crows' chorus,
he died almost seventy years later,
not knowing who was keeping watch
with a hook through his chest, curing.

RUE ST. PAUL

Boys playing at soccer in the fenced yard
cheer when the butt-hugging mini-skirt passes,
legs scissoring slowly, aloof.
Now and then one of the priests emerges
from a side door of the church, aloof, too,
his cassock barely swinging under shadow.
These mornings, Penelope wakes thinking
how much depends on another day
in the Red Wheel Barrow, and the woman
who owns the silk shop stares out her window,
her fingers grazing a paisley scarf.
Miss Manon slides another tray
of *grillés pommes* into the display
case, wiping with her bent wrist the classic
wisp of gray hair from her forehead.
Such a narrow prospect, viewed from its corner
with Rue St. Antoine, yet the bicycle
of commerce and prayer navigates it,
ridden by Jacques Tati's ghost, tottering,
its bell ringing insistently enough
to echo all the way to the river,
and in the ears of the gargoyles perched
on the great cathedral beside it, circling.

AND THEN IT RAINED

Sweating, a composition himself
in his black hat under the forgiving sun of Provence,
Cézanne began to understand how little he needed.

He made light seem immanent,
the poise and balance of matter expectant,
a hover within everything. Worlds at once.

Mont Sainte-Victoire is not a mountain;
it has folded up from the movement
of tectonic plates into his paint's stone.

Somewhere in that dance, the light in the brush,
in the folding of layers under the earth,
he saw the center of the web, an eye
as fierce as his, embedded, unremitting.

It looked back at him.

TIME'S BODY

The skybell
with neither clapper nor dome
rings.

Air draws
words into its passing,
nothing in some other
guise, time's
body.

Snow fills the bell,
gathers into its tolling,

falls.

OFFICE

The day I said goodbye to my modest
university office, I stood still
in the middle of it, door closed.

The time of day didn't register—the usual dust
seemed no more than what I had breathed daily,
a professor's legacy—but it must

have been late afternoon in the half light,
whatever that is, settled on the panes
of the influential window. I looked at it.

I looked at the ceiling, the plastic honeycomb
cover on its fluorescent centerpiece. For almost
forty years it had kept my bald head warm.

Now it became the axis on which I tracked,
not dancing exactly—I don't know how—
but turning in place, arms out like a Greek

in a taverna, my rhythmic motion
blent with the lost hours of the place, lifted
from me in the lifelong art of becoming gone.

I enlarged my orbit until I touched the walls.
I sat on the desk in passing. I swiveled
the chair. I ran my fingers through the knell

the empty shelves cast into the air.
It was a blessing I bestowed on myself,
made pure by my knowing I didn't care

beyond this strange, contained farewell
which was also a greeting, a blending
of selves and time, not a eulogy or a toll

but a toast. I stopped, back in the center,
set my hands in a steeple under my heart,
bowed. Then I opened the door

quietly, the one I had passed through those years
ago, and through those years, only the one door,
and left, taking back all my entrances.

GREENBRIER FOREST

He keeps coming back, holding it together,
a sketch of his self. The oaks and hemlocks
across Hart's Run show only a mottled light
even at midday, held in the shadows,

a sketch of themselves as oaks and hemlocks
might become, no matter the perspective.
Even at midday, held in the shadows,
the self may merge its disparate layers,

might become, no matter the perspective,
a focus of its own surprise at being.
The self may merge? Its disparate layers
aren't trees or understory or a creek,

focuses of their own content at being
what they are. Yet the place he comes back to
isn't just trees and understory and a creek
he loves for their own sake. He imagines, too,

what they are as the place he comes back to,
inspired by light, defined by shadows, shifting.
He loves for his own sake, too, imagining
himself as he is in the place he dreams of.

Inspired by light, defined by shadows, shifting,
he becomes whatever merges when he sees
himself as he is in the place he dreams of.
He keeps coming back, bringing it together.

GRATITUDE

Such a fine morning, the light gathered,
Air lifting in the Japanese maples,
Nests of shadow in the pines.
Darkness fledges, misted. You bow to your book,
Replenishing before the day scatters
Around you, giving, less sensible returns.

Slowly we drift into ourselves,
The body's discomfort being.
Unless some miracle transforms us,
All we know is our knowing, and it fades—
Renewal of another kind, a leaving
Turned inward, light blowing itself away.

GRAINS OF LIGHT

The old man at the railing
above the boy leaves his body
and perches lithely on the bannister.
A tinge of mischief and delight
suffuses him; he is an aura
in himself, an implication.
Though the staircase is in three
right-angled sections, he slides
down the bannister as if it were
one smooth grain of light
and he the breeze enlivening it.
Not for an instant does he tilt.
The boy watching him from the doorway
beside the last section of stairs
feels inside his body something
kin to the motion of the old man,
a filling, as if he were going
to meet this airy brilliance descending.
It frees him to lift his arms
and see himself depart his body,
rise toward his one true mending.
Who are we! was not a question
he put into words, but it fit
his sensation, his inspired waiting.
They didn't put anything into words,
these two affections, released to join
somewhere, eventually, in a place like this,
no place where nothing happens
that isn't a dance in air, a blessing.

FROM *TABLES* (2009)

MONKS

He bends to the manuscript blossoming
under his pen, amorphous roseate

haze rising from the gesture his fingers make,
smoke from a magic lamp even older

than the gnosis he is moved by, moves from,
inditing, word by illuminate word,

the truth hidden forever in the letters—
the very ones—he so diligently sets down.

He's not writing history—no one can
do that. He's loosing its air

into the air we breathe, trembling
with the wonder incipient in an eyelid

or the rind of a lime. He feels the fire
and dolor of his golden capitals,

the darker ages become a bursting ground,
craters of mindflame, the running crowns

of thought, essences rising
above the water where the names burn.

THE WIND SINGS, THE WIND DIES

I climbed the steps
to the stone niches above Sweetwater
Canyon, sat in one and listened
to the wind sing across its mouth.
I was a still clapper
in a bell cut into the cliff's side,
as close to no one
as the wind's dying.

Across the canyon
hawks shaved the sky
above the stark cottonwoods,
the tails mapped
in an elation of air.

Somewhere a Navajo woman
sits before her loom in the sundust,
making a pattern of all this.
Her shuttle's hush
blends with the fibers.
My absence is a thread in the weave.

KEEPING

The figure behind the railing
above me turns to my voice.
I wouldn't call to him if it weren't time.
His sienna robe settles about him.
Though he is old enough to be my grandfather
I know my face nests in the bowed cowl.
When he straightens, my exact expression
plays like a harmony
in the distance between us.
This is neither mirror nor hologram
but a keeping of each other's promise.
The flesh's absence will be no less
a fine tuning, nothing we haven't heard
before ring in the bell of emptiness.

THE WHOLE SHOW

The magician whips the bright cloth
away, showing his empty fingers
tuning themselves; on the little
table before him stands a mirror,
a bird gone from it.
In the midst of polite applause
a sound scratches from the dark
gathered in the balconies *Here*
and a clutter ensues, the theater
riddled with it. The magician,
his face pale as a dune,
vanishes under his cape,
a dry puddle on stage. Disconcerted,
the audience straggles out.
In the empty residue, space,
a black birdlike creature
lands on the abandoned cape,
kneads it, settles. There's nothing
remarkable about the eyes
it aims toward the deserted seats,
the ceiling, nowhere,
except the absence of memory.

TALKING WITH MYSELF

1 *Inclination*

It was all talk.
I see him step into the street,
anonymous in the planed light,
turn off, go his own way.
Once we were the same phantom,
teased by each other's voice
toward an overtone of being—his knack,
my need. We have passed the woman
in the slate caftan, her window seat,
leaning slightly, and the sunken man
on the corner, his sheet strewn with petals,
eyes cast away. We have mused on
and been rapt by the edges of sound,
stressed, blending—heard
by one of us, glossed by the other.
Now he walks with almost no music,
barely the soft scrape of his sole
down the last step, and off. I am
taken by him, as I am always taken.
How I follow is a matter of time,
if I follow, his footfalls gone,
our voices absorbed by themselves
toward a silence we could be blessed by.
It was a calling.

2 *Transition*

The old man's head's bowed.
He is in a place strange to him, high desert,
yet he feels he could have been born here.
He sits on a stone bench under a pleached roof.
His forearms drop loosely between his thighs,
his knees spread slightly.
He could be a man waiting
for a prayer to come to him,
or for the number of the year in his head
to turn into a hawk and fly off.
His eyes are partly closed,
the lids hovering toward a clarity.
Or shade. He is the son
of nothing, and its father,
a passage for air and light, a transition.
Words have filtered to the bottom
of a pool whose surface is expressionless
as coal—his mind, perhaps,
if we could know his mind.
If, in the long measure of life
that has brought him voices,
he hears yet another, he will cry *Mercy*
and try to draw them together, more tuning.
But if the hawk has flown,
the prayer gathered into his waiting,
he will hear not even the nothing
he had imagined, or its call.

3 *Blessing*

On a mesa an infant sits,
hardly there, almost transparent,
an inkling of himself becoming.
As I write him my pen shrinks,
these letters shy of their aiming.
He is no word. He is a thanks-
giving of earth and air knit
of his waiting and my intent.

Made of the same awe and hope,
I lift him and gaze up.
I kiss his forehead, his eyes,
cheeks, chest, belly button, the tip
of his penis, his thighs, knees, toes—
all the air his shape gives
me the honor of, the whole aspect
of this body we may live.

We float above the mesa, our
shuttle launched for its own sake
finally, adrift in a lyric
mending. Who absorbs who
in this dance, who's father
who's son, who's bearer, who's borne,
becomes the name our being whispers
to itself, our return,
the silence we gather into.

PERO THE DREAMHAWK

1 Talon

From the ledge of my cell window last night
Pero the dreamhawk took two avocados
I had set there for him. It was a bargain,
but it isn't clear what I received in return.

Pero is masterful. It is rumored
he will slash a person's forearm for no reason.
I believe this. I've seen his eye in sunlight.
It is like no other dream in the kingdom—
a talon, an archangel of a lost art.

After he took the avocados, after
he disappeared from the sill, my window
eased open even farther, seemed to drift
away and become air, become a voice
which had not spoken with clarity
for a long time. I imagined it
inherent in the air, but of this other
substance, also transparent, yet chilled,
brittle, intransigent. It would need to be broken
many times before it would be fine enough
to be indistinguishable from the air it sings.

To be faithful in a few things.
To be thankful for small favors.
To be undone by the unlikely, the modest.
To be alien in the garden, to look up.

2 *Sear*

It's tempting to say he doesn't need me,
but Pero and I are as mutual
a drift as the tectonic plates.
Without me his far cry and the kingdom
his talons mark on the sill
are hardly footnotes to the stories
of drastic awe told in the caves cut
into cliffs above the sweetwater dark.
He doesn't tell me I must change
my life, only live it, and even that
is a prehensile draw in my gut.
Speech is the shadow of a dream
between us, a dewclaw, nothing
more than the scant word I leave
for him now and then to commemorate
the bitter hour, its sear on my tongue.
He carries me into my anger
so far all of my pieces fuse
into the fierce eye of his profile,
a sealing.

3 *Stare*

Pero has no expectations.
The world is concentric around him.
He includes nothing.

It takes the rare instant
of light angling against the grain
for his eye to sharpen
its dark, singular stun.
It has the relish of a mind
bent on one thing, inward—
bare, unimpressed, a pit.

Yesterday he stared
through the dried light,
the way he flies.

He has gone hungry before.

This morning his appetite
was a scrap left on the sill.

Tonight I give him back
the same blessing, a clarity
for his throat, his calling.

4 *Vantage*

The other morning,
instead of food
I left my kachina doll, Mudhead,
on the sill.

Pero kept a distance,
watched the sun move shadows
in the vacant eyeholes.

He caught on:
there was nothing
for him to pluck out,
so he balanced on the sill
beside the statue he loomed over.

He cocked his neck.

Together they look at the world.

MONKS 2

It's a maddening habit they have,
illuminating manuscripts. I don't mean
the golden tropes that bloom at capitals

as if the words couldn't lead somewhere
by their own light, but the commentary
that runs in their minds, overtoning the text.

They would above all be clear, coax
the text clear, gentle the wispiest hint
in the quietest, most remote niche

into the open web where the mind's breeze
might ruffle it as one. Their calligraphy
in the guttering dark spins toward this,

each word wanting to join the next,
an unbroken skein for the mind to weave with,
reweave with. Troubling, a farthing dropped

in the mud. A year's drag of sciatica seen
as an offering. Drought in the refectory
garden felt as light—a discipline

inclining, a refrain. The soul designing
its shadow music, blooming through the nib.

VOCATION

... whether they listen or not.
—condition repeated in *Ezekiel*

Do you ever want to just throw it up?
I ask Ezekiel. Doesn't work for its own sake
wear you down after a while? Don't you stop
sometimes and look up at the boneless waste
and wish you could disperse into its gasses?
Yes he answers. And *no. Depends* he says.
And cancel these italics.
They make my voice look like an excrescence.
I'm unsuited for such singling out.
Anonymity isn't an italicized condition;
I'm trying to blend in, not to be called on again.
I never think of throwing it up, but I like
the image: all those bones haphazard, rising.
Think of the whoosh and whirr; talk about counterpoint!
It would outBach the whole Bach family.
And how stunning it would be for my backlog
to spray its clandestine discipline skyward.
It beats space trash, or an explosion—
Old Plum with its eye of fire—
bones in orbit, bonestars, people imagining
again, connecting, making up constellations.
The resurrection of the body! Beats
the Chebar Canal, that huge cloud of fire,
robed in a radiance, and in the center of it—
in the center of the fire—a gleam
as of amber, and figures coals burned around,
torches moving as the figures moved,
the figures themselves torches, solar, flaring.

They thrived as if fire were their element,
their cheer and relish,
the wine and vermicelli of their souls.

Here (oops) he says,
pushing a metatarsal at me. Hold this.
Think of it as a lightning rod,
a ground for forces gathering,
the most farfetched congregation
of what some other poor cobblers dug up
and strung together as the periodic table.
What we're made of.

KUNGÄLV, SWEDEN: CHRISTMAS, 1938

1

Otto Frisch was not thinking of the long-range
firefall, fallout, though for an instant
during his walk in the snow with Lise—
the two of them warmed by intimation,
the seethe of an idea, Bohr's droplet,
a dwarf dumbbell dividing—the bright prospect
of such reaction may have stunned him,
turned his mind for a spun millisecond
into its own ground zero: an image,
a shockwave of exuberance, a bane.

2

They took tea often that week, Lise Meitner
and Otto, in the small inn below the cliff.
She spilled sugar on the linen cloth
as she bore it in the miniature spoon
from bowl to cup. His fingers fretted
the woven surface as if they hankered after
the keys he was so expert with.
Families of talent, nurturing, full of humor.
Lise has come from Stockholm, her exile.
Otto's father will be released from the camp
in the new year. She walks in the snow
beside him skiing across King's River.
A pad of paper in her purse,
innocent as thought, waits for their drawings,
the rough drafts of the mind's new rendering
of the appalling core of things, of itself.

JOINTS

You strum my shoulder, as if to draw music
from the infraspinatus, the bell curve
of heft and bearing. It bows toward your hand

as a cat's back lifts to an incipient caress.
We shoulder our burdens, we put our shoulder
to the wheel, we work shoulder to shoulder;

young Atlas bore the world on his, with less finesse
and wit than one might wish, yet was able to stand
for his story. It's an odd juncture of sinew and nerve
to run your fingers along so gently, seeking music.

My friend Ezekiel roams his boneyards forever,
single-minded, serving the fundamental gist
of the joint: it not only connects this bone

to that bone both ways, it also enables
the rigid to roll and rotate, Astaire to be loose
as a goose; with Marceau and Hines on the loose

we can bear better the periodic table's
dark, imperious secrets, its ingrown
terror. At Los Alamos the physicists
danced when it seemed their work would last forever.

Some of my other friends are less immune
than Ezekiel to the whims of assembled man.
Miró's incendiary charges delight the young;

they float like particles in the eye of God,
deciduous orbits decaying with a half-life
beyond dimension, affecting if not his life

then perhaps his vision. It is, in fact, near God
Paul Klee sought a place. He would have painted on dung
had it been a more stable medium. Cézanne
painted on water. It proved immune.

Your fingers slip along my elbow and wrist and knuckle,
apparently not caring where they hang out. I suspect
they would be happy with any old joint—the back

alleys of the toes, the popliteal's sultry corner,
the sally-forth of the joint that is not
a joint, pendulous, ready or not

with its chain reactions, Little Jack Horner's
plum charged with the future. It's agaric shape lacks
the comforting, mammary swell of the circumspect
cloud over Trinity. You kiss my wrist and knuckle.

We persist: Zeke and Joan, the two Pauls and you—friends,
the present tense, our immersion in
the welter called God, the planet's roll

and rotation, nova, part and parcel, here;
lists without verbs, essence of hope and being;
red burning spits, sapience, coil of being

and essence. Where we hang out, sphere within sphere,
all guesswork, loose in the mind's infinitesimal
pitchblack scurry to counter itself. Connection
among the last extremes you'd think could be friends.

Zeke harps on that, his trials, the liminal expanse
through which he roams, humming, implying a tune
might eventually rise from his composures.

He taps you on the shoulder, smiles, complicit.
Elegant, fine-boned Laura Fermi must have touched
Enrico like that uncountable times, touched

him, too, where he thought about the exquisite
blossoming of the actinides, prolonged exposure
to which mars the fingers. Outside, I hear a loon
cry, while the universe infinitely expands.

This can be played over and over, these same notes,
these procedures, lines under compression,
moving from the mind, touched, to the fingers,

which release them into the figures of thought.
It's what fingers do, touch the imagination's music
into the world that it might be heard, music

bereft, nostalgic for the silence it issued from, caught
in its bearing signs. The most poignant singers,
hearing those origins, know life is fission.
They are—Bohr, Miró, Frisch, Joliot, Cézanne—making notes.

YUCCA MOUNTAIN

Give the plant itself a foothold
and it will *undo* a mountain.
Grows down, grows down.
Spreads out its excursions everywhere
like thousand-thumbed chains.
Is no respecter of stones. Shuns picks,
deflects shovels, is impervious to moles.
Leaves no surface signs of its campaigns.
A self-rhymed rummaging in the earth,
a fastening, a deliberation.
You'd never guess, in summer
when its white bells cluster on roadside cuts,
rendering the air delicate above
the spreadeagled spines of its leaves,
how subversive, how replete its boring,
how little water it needs to thrive,
how immune it is.
                     Over the Ghost Dance Fault
the mountain rises, a puny black spine
hardly more than a dune among the ridges
time has rifted up in the desert around it.
The borer took just two years to tunnel through it,
and then the vertical shafts to the vaults
for the spent stuff, giving *go down*
a new meaning—giving
new meaning a new meaning, making
the yucca's tubers seem a mere whim in the sand.

Lovers of the wind dancing above, keeping
the planet's time, carried all these years
the image of one fault, their ceremonies
tracing it into the air, releasing its crooked
intuition into their own rhythmic webs,
movement that lasted briefly, and is gone,
ghost of itself now. How can
they dance again their spidery weaves
when, without the slightest shifting of plates,
new plummets sprout in the wake of the great engines?
Cliffs of fall undreamed. Vibrations crazing
the music to which their bodies ribboned.

It was northeast of here a good distance
I raised my father, gave him away
into the opening mesas and kissed my self
welcome into the airs I had been making
us of, all these decades.
We left our echoes. If you go there
you can breathe them. Our heels click a joy
together. Our motions give a pattern
to their air anyone can join,
invisible leaves from a notebook flying,
ghosting our dance, feathering its voices.

REFRAIN

Robert Oppenheimer and
General Groves, post mortem

1

When they are spirits of the past themselves,
they meet, *sans* everything, hearts on fire
for nothing, all schema hung out to dry,
flapping randomly in the neverair,
items in Miró's discarded canvases.

It feels like a liberation. Why
else would they be everywhere and nowhere,
bodiless yet present, unable to speak
yet full of words in a littered exosphere
where only their non-echoes can reply

to their longing? Nothing can contradict
a wild surmise, or a fractious hint,
or a practical fitting together of lenses
by shaped explosion finding implosion out.
There was no longer a point of impact

for either conflicting theories or tenses
of personality—one a shrewd bearbrunt
bulldozer, the other a master
of withdrawal and trenchant mother wit.
They overlook their mountain's charred expanses.

In this fluttering aftermath of disaster,
boneless and blown, Oppenheimer's implausible hat
and Groves' dress brocade are as anonymous
as a dreamcatcher's feather in the void,
minuscule detritus left to pester

the stars. *What if? What if?* A soft chorus
of unstrung tunings hovers, its kinetic hum
like willow leaves floating in a soft wind.
They could be near the direst vacuum
if we could measure where they are, their afflatus

dispersed so finely in the nanoseconds
of minus time. The fall of a sparrow,
summers' fading, the bland eye of an empty
dryer, a jump rope's tick, the blade's furrow,
parching, unseeded—through these one reckons

phases in a declension. Cacophony,
too, despite itself, needs time, a mere extreme.
But Leslie R. and J. Robert lack a place
you can call a place. Their fondest dream
is no longer *fact* but *now*. Humpty Dumpty,

Ozymandias, the Seven Cities
of Troy, bog bones still hidden from old Zeke,
seem a paradise beside this feckless drift,
this rinse of neverair. If they could speak
is as extraneous as ice,

and numbers are pawns in a cosmic grift
that makes God's dice little more than jacks
thrown on a stoop. *Who would have thought?* becomes
a strain in the hanging music
inaudible but for its inmost gift:

2

the neverair sings to itself, consumes
and nourishes less than nothing falling
open and away, rangeless, the filters
of starfall, light chaining until light's all
shatters past them, meeting without words
or scheme, not even the imponderable
galactic crawl toward itself, toward fire

that boils more fire, a grace of flames
spun in the unhearkened telling
gone, webs without a weave, shelters
of windless inclination, knell
unwinding departure inwards,
a likelihood kept unstable
by its own luminous absence of air.

3

They would assert themselves.
Of course. They would light a fire
in the numberless cold. *Dry*
is an absence within air
replacing air; spaces

become space. They don't ask why
nothing ignites, why *nowhere*
is the language they speak
in the flecked exosphere
that gives neither reply

nor echo, or contradicts
their being a lost hint
of themselves, lenses
of lightfade so thinned out
you could breathe them. *Impact*

and *float* are synonyms, tenses
time's spume. They bear the brunt
of weightlessness; they master
arts that require neither wit
nor dexterity. Expanses

that once dwarfed them, disaster
looming, like Oppie's hat
become as anonymous
as a speck in their new void.
Where colleagues used to pester

them—*what if/ what if?* a chorus
of exhaustion—a feathered hum
now shadows their hearing, spacewind
just out of earshot, a vacuum
beckoning one afflatus

to join another. Seconds
vanish into it sparrow-
quick , yet it stays empty,
a bottomless furrow,
seedless. If one reckons

the mind's polyphony
as evolution's extreme
achievement, this is the place-
less place to test that dream.
Not even Humpty Dumpty

applies; the leveling of cities
is an image old Zeke
doesn't pursue: the drift
of bone dust refutes him. To speak
in the tongues of outer space

requires we bypass the gift
of sound and matter, take
to heart the fate that becomes
us, the nuclear music
ghosting the traces we have left.

DREAMCATCHER

Only God's most unholy nightmare
could ruin this—a vision, say,
of the brightest angel at the instant
of his fall, his dark germ breaking,
a mushroom parachute he folds into himself
when he lands, his putrid fire
burning only the eternal cold shoulder
he shrugs at life. A nightmare like that
might clog this fine mesh, shatter its rim,
consume the house and the air of the house
and the people who live in it.

Angling itself toward the dream's drift
that would escape it, this dreamcatcher,
matchless, hangs in the north bay
of the sleeper's bedroom. Its chamois-wound rim
encloses a mesh of arcs, intricately
interlocked, like the wings of a band of angels
seen from above, a la Busby Berkeley;
their tensions and resilience resemble
those of a well strung tennis racket.
It's four inches across. Three tiny drops
keep their suspended orbits in the net:
one turquoise, one quartz, one silver, all
dancing round the little wedge of malachite
at the center of everything, marking the point
where the best dreams gather, to be dreamt again.
Small beads and feathers dot three rawhide stems
spilling like a beard from the lower edge.

Were this inestimable sifter hung in the long wind
of space, it could tilt and waver for centuries
and pick up nothing of measure. Here its life
riffles with the sleeper's breath, his dredging,
his endless turning among the sortless dreck
that keeps his mind a continual fission.

The sleeper murmurs to himself: he has
a sense of how far darkness radiates,
taking care of its own. It troubles him,
his sleep. The dreamcatcher, settled,
picks up the smallest wisp of dismay,
of possible deflection from the arcs
of joy he would follow, releasing it
into the smoke and mirrors beyond
its absorption. Through the window at night
he sees stars, pieces of the Big Dipper
but nothing else he could cobble together
into a clear shape. Sometimes when he looks through
the dreamcatcher he can't tell the drops
from the starscrabble, his pupils relaxing,
his vision becoming the mesh, the angel wings,
the best dreams shimmering in the malachite.

BLACK HOLES

A tour of the gallery

All the yonic yawns that inhere in this subject
belong to other ruminations and will not appear here.
Instead, the poster says, observe the various torques,
molecular time,
compression not even the most
accomplished lyric poet guessed,
how the universe forks
and forks, spills into itself, and doesn't rhyme,

how the ghosts take forever to appear and disappear,
leaving nothing but whispers that lead us to suspect
and nominate and theorize
about what might have been there
once, and isn't. Attraction one,
a series of gaseous centers
drunk with light, shows the sure sign
of a black hole is its bright enterprise,

its dazzling maw, a galaxy's digestive tract
consuming and belching, all process, a plummet of sheer
combustion. In the adjacent aisle
Centaurus A
tilts in its homey
approximation of an eye
stitched out with vitreous
floaters, spider style.

Next door, Andromeda, flanked by two satellites,
presents its pale yolk and sizzled fringe, a cannibal
dying of its own appetite,
the drastic, crawling fate
even of the sweet Milky Way,
its Orion Arm nestling the planet
we are nourished by.
The rest of the display—

Berenice sleeping, Carina, Whirlpool,
Dorado, Sculptor, assorted classical acts—
overwhelms the diminished visitor
of the species we are most
fond of, leaving it lethargic,
disoriented, at the core
burned down, a depressed wreck
capable only of staring at ghost

images flickering on the front of a box.
On my wife's sewing machine bobbin and spool
feed their needle, its slow
and rapid tickings making a rhythm
less predictable than Penelope's
at her loom, but a constant flow
nonetheless on the wide fathom
of space's deep entropy.

The TV screen and the stitching are both hypnotic;
the wayward sailor's wife remembers to exhale
as her shuttle slides through the warp,
and she can undo what she does;
from the machine a hemmed panel
of bright cloth eases—so our sleep
sews memory and dream, the rise
of being. Nothing is final

but repetition, the rehearsals of appetite
and gravity spinning and spinning in neverair.
Name the new names, conjure
umbrellas where there is no moisture,
bless the monks' bowed gesture, evoke the magician
and his inky smoke, call up
from the drasty deep
echoes of Magog and Leviathan.

Litanies of spite
and counter spite reel and unreel;
tongues flap their blame and praise,
their coups and coos;
organs rise, beget, and melt
quicker than sighs.
It's as silent out there among the cataracts
as generation, as the movement of glaciers.

Once upon a time before the future is a speck
of leftover cinder from our seared planet,
all the figures we have dressed
the stars and their spaces with
may peel off and drift
toward us—an instant of bare sight,
of unlending. Our eyes may devour this, impressed
at last with their own blind light.

FROM *THE MAN WHO LOVES CÉZANNE* (2003)

SOMEONE ALONE

Those wonderful rhymed lines with their metered flow,
their dependability, their planned release—
and yet it was easy to let them go.

The desert winds are irregular. They tease
and exacerbate at once. Often the ear
will fill with their fading, their inward stress,

nor is it whimsical how each person's fear
of heights, or drowning, or crowds, takes on a beat
different from anyone else's, by a hair.

Rhythm's a rhymeless word, as is poet.
What we seek in the sounding is undulation,
absorbing the winds' reluctance to repeat.

The voice breaks silence and loves the overtone,
as a diamond cutter's chisel seeks the place
where one light tap will clarify the stone.

Someone alone now listens for the trace
of a lost word time may be passing through
to a measuring of air, the mind's redress:

such is the setting where surprises play,
the winds' bemusing cadence, a shimmered grace,
for whose relenting temper we all let go.

WALKING TO SCHOOL

He never arrives.
The frame house he has left behind him
begins to disperse, to thin, verging on air;
a small dynasty of trade and the flutter
of currency in the heart fades with it,
no more than cigar ash blowing across
a flagstone porch in late afternoon.
The tan stucco building with its brick-red
terra-cotta roof and wide playground
waits roughly where I stand watching,
and is not visible. He approaches me,
or I suppose he would
were it not for his continuing suspension
there on the sidewalk, beside the hedge.
He is preoccupied, a self between.
Sometimes he pulls on a glove. Leafs
through a notebook. Seems to smile
through the way his body tilts, in motion
yet not quite walking on; so a sentence
begins its tentative course, imbuing
its own wilderness, a shape of trial.
He nods his head. He has no idea
of me, his foregone voice now beckoning.
Everything I do, everything
I sleep, waits on his tempering,
and will only with the heavy,
impeccable slowness of a glacier begin
at last to melt toward an opening for him.
Meanwhile, he continues to intend;
which arm do the books fit under,
what is the best slant for his cap?

He can't imagine how his teachers
in the stucco rooms will welcome him.
He is the kind they love to see pass
under the lintel, his eyes saying
I am why you are here; I will become you.
They will beat their erasers until
a great unison of chalk dust rises
over the poles, the seals barking with joy
and the penguins rolling their hips
and flapping their pennants over the ice.
He looks into his brown bag to see
what's for lunch, picks a leaf from the hedge.
The manner of his staying is endless
invention, carried into the most minute tic
of his shoulder against the strap
of his bookbag, or his hands' ornate looping
of one shoelace over another.
He becomes, over the still
unfolding of our mutual divide,
a measure of my attention.
Like a shapeshifter, the stucco
grammar school goes through its incarnations
until all the decades' buildings become
silhouettes and settle in to a binding,
its pages stirred now and then
by the tentative span of our longing
for one another, as if by a breeze.
He has always been tending
toward this gathering, waiting with me
to dance out of the book into time,
where the word begins.

HERE, PROMISING

Go, little books

Don't look back.
A particular place always waits for you,
set up to look like a nursery,
mobiles twisting in the air of the old voices,
sometimes broken by faces peering down.
A descent in a diving bell
into the most stringent depth, or time travel
into a stunned migration of settlers,
couldn't draw up stranger creatures for you
to gawk at. Still, lying there, you begin
the intimate gestures that have carried you
through the world, everyone's little secrets,
until, like Narcissus dreaming, you long
to look away from the multiple faces
in the water. The slow wind sometimes
ripples them, or a stone falls from nowhere,
spreading its concentric round and round
and round through their semblances.
Sometimes they look off by themselves,
or bend to books, reading pieces
of what you'd like to know, or forget.
The shimmer of loss never gone long
from such drift seems to be common ground,
and life becomes a matter of what you choose
to do with the other hand,
stirring the surface haphazardly,
playing the faces as if they were keys.
You think sometimes they are friends of yours,
friends of mine, for we displace the same air,

turning our contour into the place we speak from,
a voice through which we bring, sometimes,
all our separate patchwork into the sound
of one being beyond sight,
perhaps here, promising,
perhaps light years away.

FREE WILL

William Shakespeare was
born in a ripe apple
in a seasonable month
when marmalade was dear
at any price for milady's biscuit.
As an infant
he could spit melon seeds
from a distance of fifty feet
into twilight without missing.
He knew the difference between
a cart wheel and a cabbage,
and often dribbled musically
into his mother's claret.
Anne Hathaway was
but a dream in his left eye
when he herded summer
into a teacup, and no one
could have guessed
his propensity to eels
and brass bedknobs coated
with honey. His youth
trailed him carelessly, ribbons
awash behind a sunbonnet.
Occasionally he would stumble
on confusions of raiment,
their whim and buckle and froth.
As a lover he notched
his conquests on a pistachio
shell, which he would set
beside his tankard, left
on the nattered table

at the tavern.
He never let
strangers buy his languor,
his vague drifting off
under which, like a sky,
the players played.
He was a king and a ducat,
a lamb's-wool tick and a creel,
a stress and a jackanapes,
and a folly of scrolls
to hang a tongue on.
He pillowed his head
on an idea only once,
and was seared through the
tympanum:
this is why he walked with a tilt,
swayed, and fingered nonexistent
pomegranates year-round
at the market stalls.
He grew betimes a dead-eye
with a word. He could pin time
to a stable wall, or
a derelict stranded, or
a head bent in waning.
The lone voice lost in converse
was almost everything
to him: a garden, a cast.
He has not died yet
in the ways we give ourselves
pause hereafter, and his body
of work is such a congregation

of impolitic Proteuses,
it is no more a location
than the instant of darkness
after a skyrocket fades,
or a mist of breath feathering
on a looking glass.

A SHADOW THEY CAST

The boy, an old man now, remembers
his grandfather sitting in the rowboat,
a silhouette against the skyline,
his head and torso a flecked hollowness.

His grandfather, sitting in the rowboat—
still as the wood the boat is made of,
his head and torso a flecked hollowness
as if there were leaves on it, as on the trees,

still as the wood the boat is made of—
was a piece in the boy's puzzle of time.
As if there were leaves on it, as on the trees,
the boy's memory seems to stutter in the wind.

Was a piece of the boy's puzzle of time
missing, lost in the treeline, or the bay's dark?
The boy's memory seems to stutter in the wind.
He isn't sure who is the old man in the boat,

missing, lost in the treeline, or the bay's dark—
his grandfather, himself, a shadow they cast?
He isn't sure. *Who is the old man in the boat?*
becomes the question memory composes.

His grandfather, himself, a shadow they cast,
a silhouette against the treeline,
become the answers memory composes.
The boy, an old man now, remembers.

NO WAY OUT

Tent Rocks Canyon
Cochiti Reservation, NM

Nobody lived here, or does. No *Old Ones*
pitched camp for six or seven centuries
and then vanished into speculation.
These are just high cones of erosion
leaning into the mesas they blend with,
having no relation to the names
imposed on them. The canyon's cramped
listing and angled drift make less a path
than an inclination thwarted

into switchback by falls of scree
or boulders too ample to scale.
On certain isolate cones
cap rocks teeter, irregular cartoon
toys poised on fingertips across the skyline.
They shift into view suddenly when the canyon
elbows its way out of a cul-de-sac,
and are gone as quickly in the simple
rickrack sewn here. Not even pinyon
gets a foothold in the tuff dust and stark rock.

A wren flits and burrows
its way deeper into the canyon, its song
an aural trail to follow to the last
closed corner, where one could give up
whatever's left of direction, and start fresh.
This means stop—stock still—and listen. The wren's
call fades into the whoosh of a hawk's wing,
and we're left with space itself, what we seek

in dreams of high stone where the trail entices
to its sheer dead end—to turn back
or climb the jagged edge are the only choices;
taking a deep breath in that panic despair
can be a haven. But that's just metaphor,
molecular sleight-of-mind leaving the body
to fend for itself, still solid, old rattletrap.
It's down here and, as usual, isn't ready

for what remains after the birds vanish
and the winds die away. Where's the spirit now
with its high-flown power to diminish
loneliness and stir time into a semblance
of buttress and spire? Circumstance
translates here into stones and the fissures
time carves: obdurate, exterior rings,
like nooses, circling them.

The real hawk recomposes, the height he soars
reducing him to little more than a speck
of appetite against the cobalt. The first person
to walk here, to undergo the stricture
and twist of the canyon, might have understood,
early, that abandoning expectation,
relenting to the walls and their counter measure,
gave the only passage.

             He might have absorbed
a trace of light, its particular glancing,
a soft peach tone gone into memory
without being seen, the strata's quick pattern
fretted by shadow, a tuning—
the senses of the unprotected self
opening and taking in what might sustain it
in this inspired relinquishing.

Nobody lives here, nothing's haunted—
the cones of tuff shrink imperceptibly
in the wind the hawk rides. To blend
with the canyon during one's brief way
in it, to have its acceptance of erosion
become one's own—the spirit's foregone
withdrawal from its body's dying—
is a dream less likely than another one:
to feel an inner grounding
braided with distance and an innate grief,
dusted by a faint music not its own.

HINDSIGHT

The monuments to the old heroes sink
and sink. They cannot leave the airports
or the parks, or the long avenues,
because of their fountains
and the brute weight of their horses.
Too much time has gone
into their high suspension, and they are
filled, too, with the awed gaze
of people passing, too many to count,
more even than they watched fall
on the low ground and be laid out, and marked.
The raised forelegs of their mounts
are commas in the great pause of their longing.
They look away over their cities
at columns of figures which add up
to the pitch of grief in a shoulder,
the edge of rage in fingers that would ease
the strict reins, the incipient twitch in a cheek.
They would leave, if they could—
cluck their tongues, lean slightly
in the saddle and bid their horses
turn—but where? We have given them
little or no option but to keep
their improper and reproving poise
above us on their pediments, far enough
to give them in bronze the same
improvident distance from us
they had in flesh and bone: rank.
And so, absent all other choice,
their weight bears them downward
imperceptibly, a second burial.

One day they may be level with us,
and later, in what is called *the long run*,
our descendants can look down on them
and wonder who we thought they were,
what lives they gave us that we could
hold them up so long in their departing.

HUMMER

for George Bilgere

He has held himself aloof for so long
he doesn't hear his own sound.
It seems at first a series of grunts—
dissatisfaction with Cézanne's *The Brook,*
or with the Cleveland Art Museum,
or art museums period—until closer listening
reveals the softer register, the *piano* runs
connecting the blurts, making the play
coherent. It's his own melody
wandering the galleries with him, nothing
familiar, intended for no one's ears.
Even the guards look away,
turn on their spit-shined evening pumps
and regard the floor. He sets off
no alarms, holds his arms behind him,
bent forward slightly at the waist,
as if to give his sound a better angle
on all this art, this space.
He goes from room to room
in the otherwise uninterrupted maze
of historical periods, a tracing of influence
from one century to another, himself
influential, leaving behind a trail
anyone could follow out, or get lost in
with him, creating a sort of Hamlin
with no limits but the sound barrier.
Later in the gift shop he hunkers
to the low shelves, a simmering spring
people back off from, eye nervously.

117

His sound seems more intrusive
in the smaller room among the souvenirs,
the price tags, the fat volumes of great art
bound and shelved. The Degas dancers
he serenaded on the wall upstairs
poise on a poster here, framable. He can have
a miniature of Matisse's *Two Women*
to set beside his bed, or a coffee mug
with the whole museum stamped on it.
His humming never changes, never heightens
or syncopates or shows in its tone how much
he loves the place. If he does.
When he stands it is a slow uncoiling,
as if he is lifted by the sounds he makes
and sends out before he knows them, released
from the artless place of their making.

THE MAN WHO LOVES CÉZANNE

So I close this errant hand.
—Paul Cézanne

I like the curve of Cézanne's thumb,
the end of it where the world moved.
He could ease it through the air
against one side of a brush, and the brush
would seem hardly to touch anything.
Sometimes it would poise and float
as if it didn't even touch his thumb.
I like that particularly. It becomes
for me a way out of myself, and for Cézanne, too,
a way out, though the image
of the suspended brush might not have been
Cézanne's at all. It might be no one's.
I like the way the canvas and paint box
settled compactly against Cézanne's back
as he walked the road near Auvers—dusty,
one dry, focused shape, compact himself,
hugging with his inestimable hands
the upper end of a walking stick
on which he seemed to lean hardly at all.

Thirty-two years later, a little heavier
but still outdoors, on the road, dressed in a black
suit and fedora, he leans his canvas
against a rough stone wall. I like to read
of the last years at Chemin des Lauves,
of Cézanne's dissatisfaction with his work,
never getting into the paint the vision
of his eye so that Nature kept on being,

in spite of his most exquisite, deft strokes,
impermanent and impervious. Cézanne
didn't like that, or his neighbors' scorn
or coffee without sugar. He was someone
you could trust. Near the end he began
to make only little fades of color
here and there, and then—an afterthought
or a gesture of courtesy to us,
to his memory of Aix before art intervened—
he'd brush a line or two of structure in,
trace the curve of a bridge, or a stone's
face, or the flat bole of a pine.
Everything began to wash, and it rained
suddenly, the landscape and whole air
becoming water you could almost breathe.

COMING HOME

He imagined a room in a spare hotel,
with a balcony giving onto a street
lined every day with flowers for Easter.
The woman who kept them fresh
arrived before dawn, her body an inference
he drew from the motion under the thick array
of lilies, pentstemons, and bee-balm she carried.
He imagined her strewing the wilted ones
in the desert for the wind to scatter,
some settling among the ruins of farmhouses
before they dried into the dust surrounding.
As he sat on the balcony some mornings
from sunrise into the day's first heat
he looked up the street toward the mountains,
the farthest peaks snow-capped even in July;
other mornings he turned his cane-bottomed chair
and looked down the slow incline toward the village
center, the market with its awninged stalls,
the people, brightly clothed, moving in and out
of the vision which the street and its buildings
framed. From his chair in his study
in the northeastern corner of his country
he imagined this, not as a vacation
or retreat from his life, but as a way of being
into which he could move completely,
be suspended in, all of himself
but shut of accumulated attachments—
not a fresh start so much as a fresh ending.
Behind him in the room a ceiling fan stirred
lazily above a single bed, and a wardrobe.
When it rained he brought the chair from the balcony

into the room, a moveable station,
the way one might complicate perspective
or shadow the change of seasons.
He imagined eating one meal a day,
in the hotel or on the patio
at the cantina beside the fruit stand.
Nights he walked, and became familiar
to the villagers and the owls, and himself.
Imagining little, he received more
than he could have imagined.

                               Native to a place
altogether different, he packed one bag,
a carry-on with a few changes of clothes,
and took a series of diminishing planes
southwest to somewhere matching his mind's drift—
unwound from a skewed taxi, registered
at a spare hotel, moved the cane-bottomed chair
onto the narrow balcony, sat, and looked out.
Uphill he could see a nettled graveyard
where a ragbag of a woman pulled a goat
through the tracks of staggered crosses.
They lifted the dust into swirls and little columns
that held their shapes an instant, and fell away.
He felt the vision brought an entitlement
he had no access to, and drifted off
into a revery in which he was
dispossessed even of what he had lost
and neglected to notice. Toward the village the wind
tousled food wrappings into the recessed
doorways marking stages in the street's decline,
at the end of which in the blank face

of an abandoned convent there was a turning
westward past a few adobe hovels
and on into the wry and mordant dust
of everyone's design. He stayed the time
it took for expanse of desert,
the clawed mesas, and the high sky
to focus him, a small lens the accurate sun
could pass through and pinpoint dry tumbleweed.
Anywhere he stood he was a dot
invisible from everywhere he was not,
but the still eye of fire found him, isolate,
made him feel the center of the planet,
the one thing that mattered in a place
indifferent to him as to everything else.
He learned some language, could pass the time
with villagers, but his voice became
a sound such as the wind makes leaning
across the declivity of a rock,
a plaint with a hollowness in it,
pliant, fading even as it presents itself.
He sounded, in fact, like a native
and was bemused by the tentative
reduction he heard come from his mouth
and echo inside his memory,
itself a body cored of its inwards, floating
as he seemed to float, spaceless, wind-drawn.
It would not have surprised him if he'd dried
up into a slip of skin and wafted away.
Nights, walking, he would kneel by the edge
of a riverbed and go through the motions
of drinking as if there were water

123

in the river, bringing his cupped hands
quickly to his lips so not to lose
any of the precious, life-sustaining
element he had come so far to discover
was hardly there. The nobility
of it all dwarfed him, a slow dawning,
first of stun, and then a slack-jawed awe
that seemed like his soul emerging from a sleep,
a little breath after a long climb upward
toward the anticipated call of a bird
in a distance that was to be the place
the struggle abated, or a way to that place.
Logic died. So did ambition, and regret.
The woman he had watched each morning
vanished from the graveyard and the tilting crosses.
The goat nosed about, apparently
not missing the fierce drag on his neck.
Thunderheads began to mass in the west
toward evening, causing shadows
on shadows—new configurations of dust—
but it didn't rain. The hotel staff disclaimed
the small cluster of bougainvillea he found
nestled into his pillow after a night's
wandering among the foothills. He wanted
whatever forces had kept him here regardless
his mood or tendency, to keep him here,
to surround his will and energy as air
surrounds a body, to become his stress
and liberation, the place he lived.
Or thought he wanted that. As if seeing
an image in a piece of starred quartz—

the lines of its potential shattering
visible like riverbeds on a map—
he recognized clearly for the first time
that the facets of his life became real
only as he refigured them through memory,
the present moment being a prelude
to that. Time mattered later, embodying
itself. What sort of displaced longing
leads a man to realize where he's been
more fully than his being now
in the place he is?—not a simplification
but a centering, a settling in,
neither better nor worse but sharper, a focus.
For him to be here, he had to go away.
On one of his last days he walked uphill
to a bedraggled funeral in the graveyard.
Except for the gathered few, the village slept
in the thin, cool air of early morning,
their shutters still open to the desert.
He stood barefoot among the nettles, listening
as the priest scattered words on the bowed mourners,
their black shawls, the terra-cotta dust,
and into the new hole they stood beside.
Though ignorant of everything, he lifted
his share of the ground and tendered it
to the coffin, the bland boards lightening
briefly the darker dirt they descended through.
He seemed not to notice this reflection
or the small pattering his offering made,
already turning toward his place in the line
departing, a sympathetic group
making a slow beading against the sunrise.

FROM *SETTLERS* (1999)

GLANCE

Light touched me where I was weaving,
dusted the fibers; the shuttle moving
was like a needle through it,
stilled in it as I was stilled.

Before I thought, I looked at the light,
its drift and penchant, my eyes loving,
but would have watched it in the threads
at my hand, had I been so skilled.

WILL

At my feet a ring
appears in the bare floor.
I grip it with one hand
and pull. A section
about ten-feet square rises,
me in the center.
The house around me
vanishes. I am holding
myself in the air, a fakir
on my tongue-and-groove rug.
The rich matte finish soaks
up the sunshine like an ocean.
I must be casting
a shadow somewhere.
I comfort myself by thinking
this was at least part
of where I lived once,
but there's no accounting
for the ring. It seems
more naturally attached
to my hand than to the floor.
When the wind kicks up
we buck and sidle, my
left hand raised
like an old-time bronco
buster; then we do loops
on the tips of my outstretched
fingers. The floor at last

flies loose. I am left
holding the ring, which somehow
grows large enough for me
to slip into like a life
preserver. I tell myself
as if I were a class of children
on the first day of school,
Gravity is your friend.

GEORGE HERBERT

1

He speaks to me so that my whole
  drift gathers to his verse:
the page like a gravestone, his terse
  stanzas building epitaphs
that draw me to my soul—
  which I believe in even as the drafts
of disbelief shiver its poor tatters.

Though I am a shredding of other matters,
  distracted to smithereens,
he figures it to me: he has a means
  to rise lost to my longing, save
for his tuning of the sinews' tether,
  his windings earthward, his grafts of love.
No other poetry touches me so near

home, that homeless place, my placeless here.
  As graveyards were a school to him—
cursive dust rendering its shapes, a whim
  falling, until it kissed itself, his soul
repaired and flown—so his fit lines appear
  to me, a touchless Braille
I whisper to time turning, our little while.

2

You sing wherever the exigent will
comes on its own confounding as a stranger
and welcomes him, and they are both undone
by a mercy stranger still—
                              an empty bell
ringing its shadows in the breathless air;
a darkened threshold and a voice inclined
therein; a faint line always forming; time
wound inward and become the body's mind,
a settling troubled by its mean surprise
and tempering echoes—
                              such incarnations
riddle your song with light it could not earn,
is given as it disenchants the peace
also embodied there, the twisted savior's
shading and immanence, your signal prayer.

PALM READER

The end of my life
hops into my hand
like a grasshopper in a dry field.
If I were going to fish with it
I would close my hand
over it and place it in a jar
with some dry grass in the bottom
and air holes punched through the lid.
At dusk I would thread my hook
through its collar just behind
its curved black eye, or run the hook
up through its throat and out its mouth,
carrying a brown bubble on the tip.
Cast into the placid, twilit pool
it would twitch on the surface
as if it belonged there and could drift
until it reached the bank
and leapt back into the field
and into my hand again.
If I were simply curious
or gone into another phase
where fishing was a boyhood silhouette
and my wrist didn't remember
the rod tip's delicate motion,
I would watch it interrupt
the lines in my palm:
vaguely reptilian with its yellow-
brown armor plating, the upper leg
chevroned, the lower with its rows
of fine barbs, thin as a needle.
It could be taken for a calm,

meditative vestige of another time,
or simply an insect terrified to poise
by this alien surface it's lighted on.
I could say it looks back at me.
If I could see with its eyes
I would become a mosaic of light
and shadow, colored in some way
complementing the background I seem
to emerge from, or blend with.
I would be as still and complex
as it is, and it would live in my hand.

CHACO

Bred to a harder thing
—W. B. Yeats

1

There is no traditional symmetry here—
no belfry or crenellation,
no individual mark of an architect
leaving a name for features you could look up
in a textbook, no signature style.
There is only the nameless longing
of everyday life, the stones of its building.
But the stones changed, and their setting, as if
the pressure at hand made generations
touch and imagine with different needs.
They became more immediate through time,
suffused with a sense of tension in the wind
they had never noticed with quite this edge,
or the rain's tentativeness, or a thinning
in the taste of the water. Something hovered still
after the hawk dove, or drifted southward.
Something stayed warm after the last coal
split and dusted, and still the cold
infused them to a new depth.
They breathed what they didn't know, finding
yet another stone to set in their ringing.
Life itself became an intrusion
no one could make the right apology for,
though they lived theirs
until it went on without them.

2 *Flute*

I imagine these vanishing
water dreamers content
to draw air through the space
a tube trimmed, fingering
its light vagaries into the tones
of gloom and rue.
The music of the desert
played on their faces
in return, and sang
to them under the crammed
night sky. It makes
as much sense as any
other notion, that they
disappeared into *that* thin
air, at last drawn
into the music they
made through the dust they
danced with, under the black
and blue domes they
could almost touch.

3

Have alternate plans
    —Sign at the beginning of access roads to the canyon

First light on the mesas
catches the rust faces and deepens them,
seeming for the briefest of times
to screen the South Pass,
to fill it with its own shadow,
to make going or coming through it
the remotest possibility—
yet beyond it the plateau spreads
under the sun spreading across the plateau
all the way to Mesa Redonda.
At these moments they may have wondered
why such open, scintillant land,
over which morning moved like a hand in blessing,
was not more generous, did not give them
more for their passing and their staying put.
They spread themselves to the four points of the canyon,
built high and low, saw over and settled in,
watched with equal, specific clarity
the small stone at hand
and the ranges forty miles off.
They dominated and were dwarfed,
themselves a version of their own perspective.
They became local, which is the beginning
of loneliness and possession.
They labored. They made things.
They didn't want to be nowhere,
or in its middle, where they are.

4

It isn't the puzzle
of the slow slide of their culture
toward cruder stones, or the closed
smoke of worship, forced into the ground
as if the desert weren't oven enough by itself.
It isn't their roads, intense spokes
going sometimes nowhere to the eye,
heartrendingly direct, ending
with a more abrupt slam than a glacier.
Nor is it their famous vanishing
that compels us here, or to stay here.
It's their being now, their resident
silence—such pressure to listen
is like the rumor of God's absence beginning
its undetectable tear in the mind.
This is our own fate we are in the midst of.
It behooves us to be shy of them,
for whatever we may say could be the truth;
what matters is how it touches
and stays inside what we are given,
where we find ourselves—
like air in a balloon:
we see them borne and stretched
sometimes beyond their bearing.
But where people grind their limits
into their daily meal, or breathe them with the dry air,
or tender them to their children in their songs' tilt—
where such limits fix,
perhaps a few can nourish the whole

kin by proving them, eking out the instant
loss begins and the long demise sets its drift,
like the water in a small canteen
lasting beyond its plausible time.
One takes a drop on the fingers
and spreads it on the lips, thus.

SOURCES OF THE FLUTE

1 Bandelier

A hawk I can't see
for the tangled pines
and the roof of the adobe
shelter where I sit
lends to the air its *scree*
scree, a transient, thin
layer of sound higher
in pitch, more raucous
from its stretched throat,
than the voices
of those who once gathered
here, threaded their fine
daily mazes, and moved on.
The tourists who mill
now among their delicate
traces appear more ghostly
than they, whose absence the hawk's
cry seams into the air
we breathe. At eight-thousand feet
the climb to the caves takes
that breath away. A slow
line of the curious
marks the narrow
trail past the shade-licked
entries the old ones dug
into the rock's face,
giving in to the deeper
holds of their lives:
coverts of air bubbled

into the long cliffs where
they slept, watched thunderheads
build bright water
to the west beyond
the kivas, and coupled,
tomorrow a sure
continuous play of wind
across the mouths of their
shelter. Going up there
has brought me down, winded,
to rest from my short hour
passing among them gone
these centuries into mind.
The hawk rides its refrain.
I see
not its body's shadow
moving across the striated
spread of the canyon wall
it darkens and absorbs,
but the shadow of its call.

2 *Tsankawi*

Even in the rare
moments when the wind seems
to lapse on this bare mesa,
it moves, folding, gathering
aside to the loose forms
it never gives itself to wholly,
following no pattern or logic,

except as the bright
spontaneous shift of heat
drives and rises, a magic
made visible only
in cloudshadow across
the wrist, or the brittle stab
of piñon and scrub.
        The climb into this sheer
breathing sky
requires a death, a giving
up to the vanished ones
who gave to this bare
flat height their living:
handholds and footholds
spooned into the vertical cliff
face; switchback trails
worn so deep in the stone,
so narrowly harrowed
by the passage of bare feet,
they seem mechanically cut;
the stone itself raw white—
snowstone drifts in the desert.
Who never comes here
misses a natural heritage
bleak as Pompeii,
an open-air burial
without bones or teeth.
                        The wind
scrapes the mesa, whose level
spread bearing the weight of air
seems also lifted into it

along with the one who climbs
to stand a second in the sifting weather.
The piñon stirs, a little fluster;
a handful of dust rises,
thins, disperses. A shy draw
of breath feathers his temple.

SETTLERS

1 *Conception*

God the split second
before rain hits a tin roof,
between the first looped traipse in the brain
and the idea of penicillin,
or blood harping on return,
return, its orgy of replication—
the silence between
the halves of a heartbeat—
or the instant the sperm
plinks the ovum:
the zygote serving itself on its flat plate:
the numberless gaps where the divine
engendering plies, waits, keeps.

2 *Foetus*

So we may come to that juicy firefall
where the sperm heads in,
where the blastocyst rumbles and unsheathes
in the womb bed, a rehearsal,
nothing so much as a new sun boiling,
or a prick of magma, redyellowflame in the night.
Folding. Parting. Oblivious hopebind,
snail coiling in the salty prime.
And his eyes begin,
shadows in a cave, marbledark,
the uncolored iris protuberant
under the cerebellum's lobes,

145

which themselves behind the veined skinfilm
of the forehead loom, deepen, shine.

3 *Birth*

He just appears in my mind at odd times
out of nowhere.
He's not Christopher Robin
dragging his stuffed bear, or Pogo
keeping good cheer alive in the swamp,
but he's kin.
He would try out his slight step away
from the verge of mothers, look up,
be unencumbered in wonder
and curiosity, dawned on,
his eyes filling and emptying,
springing with lightshadow under the lids.
Willing.
I've never heard him speak,
but I believe he keeps time
in the nestle of names on my tongue,
becomes more nearly himself
accessible in the slow release
of my lifelong tuning toward him.
It's not my hand I hold out to him
but a place in my mind's opening
for his continual keeping, his arrival.

FROM *LONG GONE* (1996)

FOREPLAY

To leave behind
what has been

left behind is almost
as possible as ending

war
with war. The Grinch

curling in the fire
with Goethe and Suetonius

makes an air
to breathe as equably

as a few
million Jews

in the oven. Atmospheric
drift, continental

separation, a square-
jawed Nazarene

in the garden, setting up
his own death. History,

you old hag, if
I bend

to whisper my sweet
nothings

in your ear, kiss
your eternal

odor of ash, will you
love me

better
than yourself?

BEDTIME STORY

The man who came down from the ark
had two of almost everything,
so he fell into a protracted alcoholic
stupor. When he woke
the hair from his head and face
had withered away, but his pubic hair
had brushed out two feet, tapering,
and turned white. For centuries
one woman or another pulled
him around by this nether beard.
He assumed they were hunting for treasure.
He assumed when they found it
they would share it with him. He assumed
the exotic sensation he felt
crackling through his leash was power.
When he woke again, such knowledge
filled his head he stood up and tore
the world limb from limb, leaving only
the dust of his mouth trailing into the wind,
the language of the future reciting itself.

GULL

Cathedral Square
Christchurch, New Zealand

He lives here.
Beside him even the locals
are tourists. He preens
on the head of the statue
of the city's founder as if
it were his private toilet.
The refuse bins hooked
three feet up the light stanchions
serve him as pantries
when the crowd thins.
Right now he's eyeing me,
approaches in a series of arcs
diminishing like rows
in an amphitheater, until I feel
my back press slightly into the bench
I came here to doze on.
I'm sitting in his sights.
I'm at his feet.
They are red, matching his bill.
The gray wing feathers lying
across his back are torn
in two places. He keeps one eye
aimed at me: one dark silver
ring around a band of dead white
with a black dot at the center.
I am
a moderately happy man,
homesick for the bright diving terns

of Hampton Roads and the Chesapeake,
the rattling kingfishers of the James,
following their river bending in the sky.
Instead, a bird with targets for eyes
gives me his unblinking stare
from the dip of a drainage tile.
City Centre a sign on a kiosk says.
We have our little tableau
and then he moves his head down and in,
withdraws it into his suddenly balled
body, ruffles his feathers, vees his bill
in slow motion, and shrieks.
Is that his tongue I see quiver,
a yellow reed in thin air?
He repeats himself. The other
hundred or more gulls in the square
ignore him, go about their trancelike
scavenging as if his cry
is no more than traffic noise.
I get up, walk over to the nearest vendor
and buy lunch. When I retreat
to my bench and begin to scatter scraps
of bread and fish to the bird before me,
it doesn't matter if it's the same one
who has given me this life.
Any fool can see
he's everywhere.

FIGURE ON THE EDGE

Gillespie Beach, New Zealand:
The Tasman Sea

He looks as if he's a silhouette cut
from one medium and glued on another,
a slim print of someone's artistic finger,
a sharp nonce. The expanse
of numberless stones composing the beach—
the sea's shambles, geologic toejam—
makes a wide strip at the bottom.
He walks on it.
The sea and the sky are close enough
to what one usually expects
in photographs, or at the shore,
to be taken for what they look like:
curled surf, the clouds dazed in light.
There are two places to go, then,
either toward the implacable line called
horizon, which no one reaches, or
into the other depth, the flat dark
that is the man walking
on the flat dark of the beach,
feet and stones lost in it,
the outline of his body forming
the only space he could fall into.

STAYING IN TOUCH

1

I have fallen
in love again.

It's the same woman
I last

skated onto thin
ice for. It's always

the same one. She
lives in the blind

hole at the center
of my left eye, the same

place the shadow
waits

for the body
that will cast it,

the same place all
the lost shatters

of light sizzle
and fuse.

2

But it's not the same
woman at all,

just some dotty
old skew-legged

trooper who laughs
at everything. I

kiss her on the nose
and she melts

into me for the big
ecstasy. It feels

like a burlap
sack full

of carburetors. My hips
grind. Both eyes

decide *What
the hell* and my whole

field
of vision

becomes a beige
shimmer.

3

Afterwards neither of us
smokes: two

beached walruses
drifting

toward the great shore.
Her lips

flibber as she
exhales, an overture.

Already a little rheum
squeezes from the corner

of one eye, spreads
into the creased

skin. I throw
caution to the winds,

reach out and
wipe it away.

GRIEF

It is the way into the self.
—Nietzsche

It's a short road that goes on forever.
It makes a single turning.
I die traveling it, passing again
the few houses I've always passed,
filled with the same few people.
When I learn to speak of them
I discover I'm alive
only in the speaking. What I know
as my self grows in the speaking,
but is only an echo when I talk
of anything else, or am silent.
It's an echo I hear sometimes,
but sometimes it's as far away
as my birth. The only way
to enter it is to speak again those words
I've learned from the few people
who are lost in my keeping.
They never speak.
They listen for the words
I've discovered where they live.
My trail is marked by the places
I've spoken, as by husks
of insects which have flown away.

GRUBBING THISTLE

Hunua, New Zealand
for Richard Middleton

If it had dawned on me
I was standing on the bottom
of the planet, I would have fallen off,
drifted into the atmosphere,
slipped through the seams of the dark—
lost in space, no different
from any rock careening
through its tunnel of fire toward cinder.
But the paddock looked normal enough
glistening with the spring rains of October,
lush thistle patched so thickly about
it should have been a cash crop,
like June dandelions mooning
the fields back home in Virginia.
Some of it was knee high, some staggered
in zigzag clumps, some so small
as to appear beneath notice, and all of it
bored into the ground sloped at such angles
that every motion of pulling the blade down-
hill toward my body, severing another spike
from its root, felt like a drawing
of myself forward to earth, a falling toward
to keep from falling away. Hours
I repeated that motion, learning it
by heartbeat and blade beat, leaving
a trail of little craters, until
we had cleared the hard hills of the weed.
For you balancing all day

on the steep pitch of your sheep graze
was nothing more than hackneyed routine,
but when we sat finally down,
flat shadows against the low sun,
I felt like a hump on the cheeks of the world,
borne by the inverted year, the inter-
stellar tilt of things, slipping toward McMurdo
and the old ice of the deepest South,

and was content with it.

CPSIA information can be obtained at www.ICGtesting.com
Printed in the USA
LVOW13s0217110414

381215LV00001B/127/P